Silent Strength

Silent Strength

Pat Marsh

Copyright © Pat Marsh 2005

Illustrations by Fran Flannery

British Library Cataloguing in Publication data

A catalogue record for this book is available from the British Library

ISBN 1 85852 270 6

First published by Inspire
4 John Wesley Road
Werrington
Peterborough PE4 6ZP

Printed and bound in Great Britain by
Biddles Ltd, King's Lynn, Norfolk

Dedication

With deep thanks to all who have enabled me to discover
the riches of stillness and silence: they may not have
realised the debt I owe them, but from each of them
I have learned how to draw upon 'Silent Strength'.

My poetry is born from prayer,
is in itself a prayer;
and through the tumbling of the words
onto the printed page
seeps
into the stillness of my soul
and leads me deeper
into prayer.

Contents

Trust

Resurrection

Christ in Me

Stillness

Silent Strength

Strong silence
warm silence
loud silence
loving silence

nurture me
enfold me

fill me, still me
write your will in me

align me

with the sacred unity.

Lord of the Evening

Colours of evening
paint the sky,
open my eyes
to see
beyond myself.

Sounds of the evening
still my soul,
sharpen my ears
to hear
within myself.

Peace of the evening
embrace me now,
draw me closer
to yourself.

Lord of the evening
meet me
here.

Simply Be

Lord,
thank you that you're here,
so intimately close
I could not see you.

Why did I search
so restlessly?

Remind me anew, Lord,

how to simply 'be'

and there

find you.

Blessèd Stillness

Stillness, blessèd stillness

wrap yourself around me
as a warm
enfolding mantle,

wash repeatedly over me
in recurring waves of love;

draw me ever deeper
into jewels of communion
in the depths of my being,

into stillness, blessèd stillness

where I am one
with you.

The Hollow of your Hand

What's that you say;
you hold me
in the hollow of your hand,
wounds gouged out by love
embrace me still,
those nail prints
the perfect shape to rest in?

The hollow of your hand
should feel the safest place in all the world to be,
if only I could rest there

but I wrestle, fidget,
toss, turn,
pick up my own agenda
instead of nestling into yours,

until slowly,
almost imperceptibly,
after a very great deal
of effort

I still myself

in that holding place

and as my dead weight
fully relaxes
into you

I change,
grow still,
begin to feel myself
in harmony with you,

your pulse
beating, resonating
in me, through me

the mystery of the divine
becoming one
in me,
whilst I am resting
in the hollow of your hand.

A Whisper of your Love

I bring
the chaos of my jumbled thoughts
to you in prayer;
thoughts rattling round in my head
like marbles in a tin,
crashing, banging,
vying for attention
as I haltingly, falteringly try to let them go.

I long
to settle into stillness

but intrusive thoughts collide
and crash
and make me wonder if I have the patience
for this time in prayer,
until,
when all seems lost ...
quietly, unexpectedly
into the noisy confusion of my thoughts
breaks through
a compelling, beckoning whisper
of your love.

Soft and gentle
tenderly whispered

your love
floats down to me
like billowy duckling down
carried on a summer breeze,
like the fragile beauty of butterfly wings
or the treasured fragrance of an autumn rose;

a whisper of your healing love
caresses me
washes over me, holds me tightly
draws me further
into the comfort
of the strong, enriching silence.

Stained Glass

Like a golden thread
running
through the plain grey fabric
of our everyday lives,
the power of God's love
shines through the darkness;
shines on the weak,
shines on the suffering.

And where it rests,
quite unexpectedly,
beauty is uncovered.

Within the chapel walls,
the powerful play of sunlight
upon mediaeval images
of holy scripture
makes delicate highlights
of softly muted colour
tumble and dance in rainbow confusion
across the plain grey flagstones of the chapel floor.

And in this moment of surprise
the senses awaken
to the soft and subtle blend of rainbow hues,
born from a powerful shaft of sunlight.

The power of the light reveals an unexpected beauty.

But only with the sensing of that beauty
do we become aware
of the power
of the light.

The inner peace
which radiates through
from those
on whom God's love has fallen
awakens us anew
to the power of that love.

Without the love,
there would not be the beauty.

Without the beauty
we might not recognize the love.

Words Unwrapped

Lord, remind me again
that prayer
doesn't need
to be wrapped up in words,
though it's equally good
when it is.

On the days
when I'm just dead beat,
or pain has me trapped in its snare,
in the moments
when words don't come easy,
please set my mind
at rest:
convince me
the torment I can't convey,
the tears, the fog,
the weights pressing down on my mind,
have just as much significance
when placed into your hands
as all the fine words
I might wrap the feelings in
or all the conversations
I could share.

As lovers
sitting side by side
caress and hold the other
in the intimacy of silence,
help me to understand
that words
are often not required,
though I might feel the need
to voice them.

Just being quiet with you
can be enough;
can be as great a prayer,
as deep a loving:
be infinitely precious.

Give me the confidence
to know
that it's unreservedly okay
to simply sit with you,
just as I am,
and you
will do the rest.

Still Me

In the turmoil
of this complicated life, Lord,

still me;

return me for a moment
to the silence
at my heart:

draw forth
from my deep still pool of inner quiet,
draw forth
your overflowing love.

Still me, Lord:

still me
anew.

Emptiness

Waiting

I am
waiting:

waiting for God
in the stillness,
drawing near him
with faith,
sheltering
beneath the shadow of his wings,
letting him hold me
very tightly;

content to wait
and pray
and be with God,

content to 'be'
as I wait.

Forgive

Where is my God

when I need an answer
to the torturing questions in my head

when the thoughts reverberate
so loudly
in my fragile mind
that there is
no quiet space
in which to hear
his gentle, still, small voice?

Why can he not break through
this great cacophony of sound
to speak to me,
to heal,
to lead me on ?

ക്കക്ക

Be still, my child.

Be still
with me.

Let me weave
my thread of peace
across your tired and tangled thoughts.

Listen in the quietness
as I look on you
with love.

Hear my gentle whispers say ...

forgive.

Naked

When,
in the stillness,
I am stripped
bare
of the need
to keep going,
the requirement to pretend
that all is well,
the desire
to show I'm coping;

when I am stripped bare,
totally bare,
naked, as it were, before God,

all that remains is sadness
and a very great
tiredness

and God:

God holding me,
God loving me.

God.

Fractured

Where is my God

when it hurts too much
to even cry;
when my pulsing head is heavy
with a tiredness
far beyond the chance of sleep,
and the tangled threads
of my emotions
are pulled and stretched
beyond their natural limits
to the edge, the very edge,
of breaking point:
when they're locked
so tightly knotted in my head
that I dare not, dare not
even try
to let them go
for fear they may explode
and scatter shrapnel fragments of this pain
to wound and damage
others standing by?

Where is the love of God
when I am broken
with the heavy grief
of this poor, damaged, fractured life?

Where is his love
when I need him so?

৶৶৶

I am here, my child.

I am with you now

and I weep,
I weep with you.

Courage

Fret not.
Fear nothing, child
for I am always by your side
and I am specially close to you
in moments when you feel that I am not.

My love surrounds you
and supports you

always

and though that may be hidden
in the busyness and turmoil of your days
in quiet moments
when you let yourself just 'be' with me,
just simply 'be',
all shall be clear

and you will glimpse,
just glimpse,
a measure of the deepness of my love and guiding power,
an awesome strength
which only wills the best for you
if you but slow your rhythm to a calmer pace
and simply
seek my help.

For I am always there.

Don't shut me out
through fear, or ignorance, or pain.

Come – welcome me.

Allow yourself to come becalmed
within the gentle rhythm of my love
and let me lead you quietly through each moment
of each day,
where I may set you free
and give you inner peace,
a peace so great you will not
comprehend from where your courage comes;
courage to cast out fear,
courage to trust in me
and, greater still,
the courage
to be yourself ...
all your lifetime.

Don't ever Doubt

Oh, precious child
don't ever doubt my love for you.

I love you with a love
immeasurably great

wider
than the wide immensity of sky,
more fragrant
than the heady scent of summer flowers,
unfathomably deeper
than the deepest sea

such is my love
for you.

I hear you ask
where are you
in the suffering and the pain?
Where are you
in the cruelty of this world?
And where,
where are you in the disappointments, Lord?

I am the Christ you see
in the face of your hurting neighbour
and the one whose feet you wash
as you reach out
to those in need.

I am the Christ
who understands
exactly what it feels like
deep inside the agony of the pain.

And in the suffering
of your own self
mine are the everlasting arms
which hold you through.

Don't ever doubt
my love for you.

Struggle

Psalm 139.4

Lord,
you know
every single thing I want to say
before I even speak it,
you are the thoughts within my head,
the coming to birth of my words,
you are in the agony, the despair, the pain
and you will be
in the healing.

So take it from me, Lord:

take all that I struggle to voice,
all I feel incapable of describing,
everything I long to articulate
and all this muddle of my pain.

Take it:
take it from me, Lord.

I give it over
to your healing.

Take all the questioning urgency,
the striving for solutions
in my head.

Give me the grace
to accept things
as they are.

Give me the faith
to know
the answers will unfold
in stillness;

only there
in the deep still silence of eternity within
will I begin to know
your will

already written
into me.

Enigma

Selfish free will
pits itself
against magnanimous love
in a permanent tension
inside
the disunity
of the universe.

Love allows
that we should have free will:

the paradox
is that free will has its finest hour
when choosing to surrender
to forgiving love.

Free will
versus love divine:

they were never meant
to be on opposite sides.

Alignment

God Indwelling

God beyond all space
God outside all time
God without me
God within me
God the mystery at the heart of me

God the stillness
God the energy
God the pulsing heartbeat of the world

God indwelling
indwelling in me

make me one
with you.

Positioning

Psalm 18.2

I want to put myself, Lord,
where I may always be
not in the shadows of fear
or pain, or doubt,
but open,
open to the outpouring
of your love

and when all seems shaky
in my life, Lord,
I want to be standing on that solid rock
that helps me to remember
from where I gain my strength.

I want to be, Lord,
just exactly
where you want me to be.

Release Me

To be true
to my inner self,
to be all
that you might long to be in me;

Lord, this is my desire.

Release me, Lord,
to be
the me

not of my dreams

but of yours.

Discord

Friend, creator, father

you
who are the pause between my thoughts,
the gap between my words,
the energy
in the spaces of each cell,
the resonating presence
at my core,
the sustaining silence
deep within,

bring me back in harmony
with the still peace
at the heart of me,

align me

with yourself.

Strip Me

Ephesians 4.22

Indwelling God
come to life
in me

colour my reactions with forgiveness

hide my prejudice
behind your love

overthrow my hesitations
by your grace
and let your peace
drown out my fears

break through my humanity
with your holiness

and strip me

of all that holds me back
from letting you be
the Christ
in me.

Featherlike

Lord,
make me as a feather
on the breath of God,

open
to the movement of the wind,

willing to surrender
to strongest gales of your directing,
softest whispers of your grace.

Carry me on breezes
of love
beyond all gentleness.

Lift me into flight paths
that transcend imagination,

propel me
along currents of your will.

Let me soar, wheel, fly,
dance in celebration.

Let the Spirit carry me,

empower me
for you.

Ask, Seek, Knock

Matthew 7.7

Lord,
save me from the arrogance
of thinking I can manage
on my own,
can do it all myself,
unaided,
self-sufficient,
without you:

for that's what stops me asking ...
this stubborn, misplaced pride
that says I ought to be able
to do things on my own,
under my own resources;
not only 'ought',
but 'want'
as well.

But what a waste
of the vast empowering you offer me

if only I would ask.

And as I seek,
remind me
it can never be a fruitless search,
for, before I even start
you are already
seeking me,
placing yourself in situations, people, words,
places where I may find you.

And when you say
knock, and the door will open,
you omit to mention
that it's already swinging on its hinges,
just waiting
for me to find the courage
to push it wider.

Ask. Seek. Knock.

So straightforward,
if only
I could let go
of misplaced, self-sufficient pride.

Motivated by your Grace

Lord,
motivate me by your grace;
let forgiveness
kick resentment
out the window,
soften the hard edges of my anger
and give my pride the boot:
replace self-interest
with concern
for other people,
and help me to take the initiative
when you show me the need:
enable me
to always go the extra mile
for you.

Lord,
let me be motivated

by your grace.

Trust

Let Go

It matters not how distant, far away, I seem to you;
how hidden,
inaccessible, behind the turbulence of your thoughts,
how much you doubt and question
whether I am here.

I hold you still, my child.
I hold you always
in my hand.

So trust
in the darkness,
trust, in the loneliness,
trust, in the fear:
let go of your innate desire
to fight each desperate battle
on your own.

Let go

into me;

relax

and let me help.

Can you Believe?

Can you believe
that at any time,
any place,
anywhere in the world,
anyone
can have a personal chat,
a one-to-one,
direct communication
with the creator
of the universe?

He's not remote,
not locked away behind some grand protective door
marked 'Head of Operations'.
He's not tied up in meetings
too busy to listen
or to care
and you don't need to make an appointment
(though Sundays are very popular).

He's always accessible,
available twenty-four hours a day
seven days a week
fifty-two weeks a year
for the whole of your life.

And before you've even thought about
contacting him
he's heading towards you
expectantly.

Can you believe?

Desert Flowers

Isaiah 35.1

Even the desert
will blossom with flowers.
That's what you tell us, Lord.

And in some most desolate
and inhospitable places of this earth
that's how it sometimes is.
In parched, infertile ground
made thirsty for water
under an unrelenting sun,
in your season and your time
a great technicolour spectacle of flowers
bursts forth with unexpected joy,
surprising the desert landscape
in which it has its roots.

Unlike that multicoloured carpet
on that hardened sandy floor,
for us, it's maybe different, Lord.
Often your miracles creep up on us quietly,
on tiptoe as it were,
without theatrical drama,
emerging in your way, your time,
and taking us, quite frankly, by surprise.

Forgive us, Lord,
the times we thought you had forgotten us,
the long and barren months of waiting
when we simply failed to see
beneath the surface of our lives
the quiet, unhurried unfolding
of your will.

The flowers in the desert, Lord,
know all your ways.

In your created world it's not unusual,
that period of waiting in the dark;
a time when all seems dead,
when absolutely nothing
gives a hint of what is happening.
But in those parched and barren times,
seeds are scattered, roots are formed,
the promise of your beauty
germinating in the dark.

Lord, thank you that you help us
to be patient in the dark.
Thank you that you help us
to wait on you, in trust.

With clarity of hindsight
we now can see that after the desert waiting time
the time of flowering comes.

Lord, germinate the seeds
that you have planted in our hearts.
Bring forth a great explosion of your joy.
Together help each one of us
to grow as you would wish.

Unfold your great creation
through our lives.

Trust

Trust is a patient waiting
when our prayers appear unanswered.

Trust is a hidden promise
in the deep still centre of our heart
that the reassuring hand of God
is ever near
and that he longs
for nothing more
than that we should
reach out
to him
in simple trust.

Gossamer Trust

Lord, sometimes I realize
that the trust I try to offer
is actually so slender,
so fragile within me.

I desire it
to be as strong as the strongest tensile steel
but all too often
it's as prone to injury
as a delicate gossamer web
because the gut-feeling trust
that brings to birth the powerful 'yes' in me
battles unendingly
with the fears that make me doubt
my human limitations,
with the past experience
that jogs my memory of some previous defeat.

Earth my trust in you, Lord,
root it
in the depths of me
with unswerving surety
that you are right beside me
in every doubting, faltering, wavering moment,
that you are whispering:

here I am

let me work in,
live through
you,

let us be in this
together.

That Close

Draw near with faith.
Approach the sacred mystery
of this holy table
with reverence and awe.

Bow down
in simple wonder.
Gaze on the tender compassion of Jesus
and be aware
that in the sharing of these
blessèd gifts
you too
and all who feed
at this Communion meal
are called,
invited
in this holy moment,
to be the favourite disciple.

Reverence the wonder
that he holds you in such love;
amazing love,
compassionate love,
love indescribable
flowing through each fibre of your being.

Let your soul awaken
to the closeness of his love.
You too can be as close to him
as the favourite disciple,
your head on his bosom,
his arm around you.

That close.

You are that close to him
and he to you
not only in this holy sacrament,
this blessèd meal,
but always.

Unfolding

Bread of heaven
living in me

feed me today.

Help me to grow
as you have ordained.

Unfold your will

through me

today.

Cradled

Written in a quiet chapel

Here
is a peace
that cannot be defined,

a love
that cannot be contained,

a stillness
that reassures me
I am cradled in his love.

Resurrection

Alignment

Lord,
I simply desire
that my life
should reflect your love,
my feet
walk in your footprints
and my lips
speak of your praise.

I only desire
that my strength
should come from the cross

and above all else
that my will
should be in alignment
with your will

always.

Centrality

Lord, it's far from easy
to explain
to those who do not know you
the absolute centrality
of the cross
within my life,
indeed, from time to time
my logical-thinking, articulate brain
struggles with that truth.

It's only
in my heart knowledge,
my deep
gut-feeling knowing,
that I recognize
beyond all chance of doubt
that Jesus Christus
died
for me;

a loving man of peace,
incapable of wrong,
nailed to a cross as a common thief
in that once and for all
redeeming death,
redeeming act of love:

central

to the purpose of his life,
to the future of the world.

Arms Outstretched

With arms outstretched
you gave yourself,
the whole of yourself.

Man on the gallows,
bowed and bloodied,
you gave yourself
for me.

With arms wide open
calling me,
inviting me,
you stand before me still

challenging me,
inspiring me
to live my life,
the whole of my life,
to live my life
for you.

With open hands

just as I am

I come.

Gnarled Old Trees

Gnarled old trees
lie broken
and dead,
struck down in their prime,
no longer bearing fruit
or growing
through the cycle of the seasons.

Yet in their brokenness
is beauty,
timeless
weathered out beauty.

It was their time to die,
for in their dying
they sustain the life of others.

A honeycomb grows
deep inside the hollow,
bringing sweetness to the death.

Butterflies dance
around the textured bark.

Lichens and mosses
root in the crevices;
new life
where once the sap did flow.

Heavenly dragonflies
hover.

Beauty from brokenness ...
life from death ...

New Day

Grey mist of distance,
pink wash of sky,
soft stillness hanging in air,

wing beat of pigeon,
glory tipped clouds,
freshness of dawn on my skin,

echoes of birdsong,
dampness of dew:
nature unfolds
a new day.

Reality Revealed

I cannot adequately tell you
in words that quell your doubts
how the love of God
is real to me each day,

nor can I answer
why the message of his love
revealed itself
through death upon a cross,

but real it is

and more than that

it guides me, helps me,
heals me,
lifts my spirits when I'm down.

Yes,
the love of God is real to me
each day.

The Sunset

The sunset
caresses the evening clouds
with tender brushstrokes
of delicate pink and orange highlights,
painting a subtle masterpiece
of rich and vivid hues
across the eggshell blue
colour-wash canvas
of the twilight sky.

From the great creator's palette
an incandescent glow
of soft rosebud peach
shines powerfully
through the dark and brooding storm clouds,
with drifts of glorious candyfloss pink
and duckling feather lemon
tickling and teasing
the underside
of the deep, dark
cumulo-nimbus.

A storm approaches.

But
in the lull before the storm,
for a brief moment,
as the daylight drifts sleepily
into darkness,
a beauty unimaginable
awakens the senses
to the glory of God.

Resucito

Resucito!

He is risen

and he makes his home
in me.

I do not have to invite him,
implore him,
or beg him enter in.

He is
already there.

Within my vulnerable, wounded self
the Christ has made his home,
fulfilling divine destiny
through my inadequate
humility.

Infinitesimally closer is he
than I could ever
imagine.

Resucito. He is risen.

He is alive.

I am alive;
no longer I,
but Christ in me.

Imagine

Imagine your best friend died.
Imagine he gave
his life
to save you:

picture
how you'd feel.

I expect
you'd feel a debt,
a powerful sadness,
a wish to preserve the treasured memory
of your special friend.

I imagine too there'd be a hole,
a great big yawning, gaping hole
in your life.

There'd be anger too
and pain,
a pain that seemed too deep for words.
There'd be shock;
an awful dreadful numbness
and an overwhelming,
damning
sense of pointlessness.

Imagine your best friend,
your very best friend,
died

for you.

Now imagine, if you can –
a difficult leap, I know,
but just imagine
if you can –
that he could be beside you
every day,
not in a bodily way
but deep within:

imagine
a deep inner knowing
within your heart
that the spirit of his friendship,
spirit of his love,
still lives in you.

Imagine
that, though your friend has long since died,
in spirit he is still with you;
loving you,
listening to you,
laughing with you,
sharing all your hopes and dreams,
empowering you through life.

Imagine the joy:
imagine the intimacy
of knowing all you have to do
is talk to him
and he'll be there with you.

Imagine ...

Christ in Me

In Me

John 14.20

The greatest gift of all,
the one almost
beyond my comprehension,
is that
    Christ
       is in me.

*I am in you
and you are in me.*

How humbling to acknowledge
that he has freely chosen
to make his home
in me.

How wonderful to realize
I am equipped in every way
for all that I might meet,
through him
in me.

He only desires
that I should let him live
through me.

How simple.

How difficult.

How often I fail.

If the Christ

John 1.39

If the Christ were here before me now
his heart would look on me
with such unwavering love,
his gaze enfold me
in forgiving peace,
his countenance beckon me
to respond

and in the still pools of his steady eyes
would be a look of deepest longing,
a holding embrace
that longs for me
to want
all he desires to do in me,

a look that says
please come, my child,
and let me work in, live through, you;
let me enable all I may accomplish in your life,

let yourself
be totally mine,
fully, wholeheartedly, without condition,
unreservedly mine.

Come.
Come and see.

Comfort Zone

Lord,
when I'm wavering again
lead me boldly
outside
my comfort zone of faith,
over the boundaries of the safe, familiar
into the unknown territory
of loving without condition;

help me to step
beyond my known and tested limitations,
reach out
to those whom I shrink back from,
look into the eyes
of all from whom I would divert my gaze
and listen
with holy listening
to those who need to talk.

Challenge me
to reach out
to strangers who are not yet friends,

empower me
to live beyond my doubts
until I risk the joy
of letting my loving
become more like yours.

Help me to dare to trust
that I can be
the incarnation of Christ

today.

By his Grace

2 Corinthians 4.8-10

From every angle
pressed by troubles,
crushed
but never broken,
though sometimes inches
from the edge.

Perplexed
but not for quitting.

Abandoned, lost;
adrift within uncertainty
but knowing
God is there.

Knocked down again
but dusting off my knees
and bravely getting up,
enabled by his grace.

Sharing in his death
that I might show
his life,

uplifted
by his grace.

Responsibility

John 14.20

Christ
is in me
and I
am in him.

Once I've surmounted
the miraculous wonder,
the sense of empowerment,
the sheer incredulous joy,
once my heart has come, parachute-like
back down to earth
I realize
that parallel to that wonder,
in direct proportion,
runs responsibility.

To know
that the Christ
lives in me,
that the love beyond all other loves
chooses to witness to the world
through me,
is gift beyond imagining

and gifts, like friendships,
are for sharing.

This knowledge
is for sharing
but with discernment, love and care
in a way that attracts
not alienates,
heals, not hurts,
forgives

and frees.

This gift, this Christ,
he is for sharing

responsibly.

It is not I

It is not I
who looks on you with love
but Christ
who lives in me,

nor is it I
who speaks to you in peace
but Christ
who breathes this gift through me.

It is not mine,
the strength that holds me through,
but that of him
who hung upon the cross

and it is not I
who listens as you share your pain with me,
it is the Christ
embodied in my listening heart.

But it is not he

who struggles to forgive,
but rather me
who fails to let forgiveness freely flow

and it is not he who angrily reacts,
but the part of me
that fails to let him live.

It is not he
who criticizes, scorns or mocks
but sadly me
who fails to let the Christ in me
embrace you with his love.

It is not I
who sometimes walks so peacefully
through the turmoil of this life.

No, that is he,
the Christ,
living,
living in me.

My Everything

John 14.20

Dear God,
you who are my source, my strength,
my everything,
how moved I am
by your love for me.
I bow down in humility
before your majesty in all creation.

I am in you
and you are in me:

what empowering,
what wonder,
what infinite simplicity and ultimate complexity,
enigma, paradox,
love.

In the stillness, below the clashing of my thoughts,
you are there,

in the questions, vying for attention within me,
you are there,

in the feelings, tugging at my heart strings,
there too I find you

and in the blankness
when my thoughts go on strike,
you are there.

In the skipping of my heart, the singing of my soul,
the soaring on the thermals of delight
you are with me.

In my waking, in my sleeping,
in my questions, in my certainties,
in my confusion and my clarity
you are there;

always, you are there:

my source, my strength,
my everything.

Affirmation

Lord,
with all my heart
I love you,

with all my senses
I stand in wonder
before you,

with all my soul I worship you,

with all my being
I reverence you,

with all my mind
I welcome you
to live

in me.

Love Without End

Uncertainty

Lord, I'm not a lot nearer
to knowing your will
today:

maybe that's a continuous search,
an unresolved enigma,
something we never fully understand
before eternity.

So, I'm not a lot nearer
to discerning what your will might be
today

but I do know
how very much you love me.

Let that be enough.

Unworthiness

Father God,
I know
you understand
I feel unworthy
to receive your love
in all its generous magnitude

and yet
that doesn't hold you back
from offering it
unceasingly,

indeed
in moments when I feel
the least deserving
you offer more,
not less;
your hands reach out
to touch, to hold,
forgive
and heal.

What mystery,

what precious holy gift,

what love.

Low Ebb

2 Corinthians 1.9

At my very lowest ebb,
when all my own resources
have run parched and dusty dry
and all my normal coping strategies fail

I can do
no other

than turn to God

in simple recognition
of my weakness, inability
to stand alone
without his help

and in that reverent
low point,
that acceptance
and that voicing of my need,

he meets me

with the deepest, longing love.

Meditation on an Autumn Leaf

I love you, child.

I love you with a love
beyond imagining.

I hold you
in the palm of my hand,
caress you
with the tender strength
of he who made you.

I look upon you
with the deepest love
as I watch you closely
through the turning seasons of your life,
lead you
through the changing colours
of your feelings.

For you are beautiful

and I love you,
every part of you,

even
the hidden underside.

The Jewel on the Cushion

A tiny jewel
nestling on the fragrance of a soft pink cushion
encapsulates a celebration
of the wonder of the great creator's hand.

There is tenderness, beauty,
joy, potential;
all these are framed within this minute snapshot
of the wider panoramic world.

Tiny rainbows of colour
reflecting and bouncing from the surface of the jewel
dazzle the senses.

Deep in the softness
of the little pink cushion
there is expectation, potential,
new life waiting to be awakened,
waiting to grow and blossom
into something
unimaginably more beautiful
and more radiant
than before.

Within the heart of each of us
there is potential
for hidden beauty
to be born:

just as God's love
transforms
the raindrop on the rosebud
into precious jewel on velvet cushion,
so God's incredible love
can change us all.

The Constant

Father, I bow down in awe
at your hand upon my life,
your presence within me,
your purposes
running like a sure path
through the littered landscape of my days.

I'm filled with wonder, Lord,
that you should reach out
to choose me
to help in some small way
in the task of fulfilling your word,
take part
in the day-by-day challenge
of the unfolding of creation.

Lord, I want to praise you.
I want to thank you
that through all my questions,
through everything I fail to understand,
in spite of all my faults and failings
which must frustrate your purposes,
through the joy
and through the pain
you
are the constant in my life;
yours is the endless love
drawing me to yourself.

Father, I bow down in awe.

I praise you.

And I offer my life
to you.

Beyond all Time

Beyond all time,
over the edges of eternity
outside the limits of infinity
such is the depth
and the constancy
of my incredible love
for you;
a love that died for you,
that welcomes you,
embraces you,
that spills out into history
for you.

Beyond all time,
I love you.

Without Reason

Love without reason,
love without end,
love beyond measure,
love, as a friend.

Love with no boundaries,
love without fear,
love everlasting,
love that is here.

Love unconditional,
love wide and free,
love without reason:

Christ, love through me.